Radio Mast Horizon

Also by Andrew Taylor

Comfort and Joy (Ten Pages Press, 2011)
The Lights Will Inspire You (Full of Crow Press, 2011)
The Sound of Light Aircraft (Knives Forks and Spoons, 2010)
The Metaphysics of a Vegetarian Supper (Differentia Press, 2009)
And the Weary Are at Rest (Sunnyoutside Press, 2008)
Poetry and Skin Cream (erbacce-press, 2004 and 2007)
Temporary Residence (erbacce-press, 2007)
Cathedral Poems (Paula Brown Publishing, 2005)
Turn for Home (The Brodie Press, 2003)

Andrew Taylor

Radio Mast Horizon

Shearsman Books

First published in the United Kingdom in 2013 by
Shearsman Books
50 Westons Hill Drive
Emersons Green
BRISTOL
BS16 7DF

Shearsman Books Ltd Registered Office
30–31 St. James Place, Mangotsfield, Bristol BS16 9JB
(this address not for correspondence)

www.shearsman.com

ISBN 978-1-84861-262-4

Contents

This book is for Rachel Smith

She Strokes Bees

She strokes bees they must know
of course we do angel mark
faded in sunshine beyond the fringe

shaded face beneath cap follow
the flight of butterflies as they seek
buddleia growing on wasteland

"What colour are the flowers?"
"Black"
"No, what colour are the flowers?"
"Black"

A keen eye spotting planes dots to me

On the telephone mast starlings gather
are they being fried slowly
or is it convenient parking?

It gets better every time we meet

Market Place

I like your shirt Andrew

During a quiet time sit cross-legged and watch the wind
        this is a good drying line
there is a short-cut through the fence

It is worth the hundreds of miles
        to hear those words to feel
that appreciation following the lunch brought from London

I like your jumper Rachel

In Winter, the City Almost Sleeps

I don't. Despite whiskey and exhaustion,
bags demand to be carried through dawn's
expanding light.

Half dreams. A blue Manhattan, while dogs
stride the Brooklyn promenade daubed with
static snow.

Nothing really exists on snowy days.

Distance and time. Speak on differing levels.
Life flows weakly through tired memories
that linger, like roots.

Darkness, blinds. Behind evening falls.
Imagine bouquets delivered to hospital beds
and Chocolate bunnies with red collars.

Nothing really exists at this time.

This correlation. Missed meetings where
I picture the "hellos" and following silence,
looks exchanged, stored.

A gold greeting. Stored as souvenir, such
handwriting that transports beyond substance.

Little Bird

with your tired eyes
and smile you put me at ease

fed by adrenalin and midday
Scotch sweat inducing walk

along the pier and all its glory
pockets weighed by pebbles

anticipation acute through
every seam as the hour approaches

comfort like the vision
of Stanley Road nineteen

years ago safe and secure
in the knowledge of your

existence

Screwdriver Work

We cover ourselves with cloth
        work until it is time to sleep

Outside your room your sister's spinning

like a bride whispering through the door
on her wedding eve to
the husband to-be   it is tradition

Gather the ingredients for manufacture
the first picture of summer

it was a May wedding blossom was confetti
breakfast in a tithe barn

evening ventilation along with low light
allows for deliberation watch the sky

a deep orange band   reflected
changes colour   allowing stars to breathe

Waiting for the Butterfly to Take to the Wing

and lead the way to
the optimist and the poet

replenish chop the cherry tree
generational reminder every 30 years

weed shaded concrete paths
light no penetration

we shall liaise next week
I'll let you get back to your cheese omelette

time to taste the house blend at Source
myself a reminder

like Chock Full O' Nuts the first time
it never fades

it lingers like Winter's determinedness
amongst the Manhattan gutters

Ice Cold Pavements

The bus hums as though its life
depends upon it fumes cloud
chilled air red lights flicker distanced

yet near enough to feel a part
of something despite it being 6.00 a.m.

This time of morning perspective
alters before the first tea of the day

if the snows arrived I'd be first
to make footprints along the beach

thinking of Clementine and Joel
and double beds alongside

rooms in Greenwich Village
Bleecker Street writing visiting
Zinc Bar setting up a tab
drinking in preparation for ice

cold pavements and the slide home
through greying slush replicating
Bob and Suze in Jones Street

if I transported to HD189733B
would I be missed?

Small Poem

If I turn left to St Pancras
       you'll be at the Champagne bar
under the gaze of Betjeman
while I drink cans of bitter
reading O'Hara
the room too large for me

breakfast can't come quickly enough
and time for tea before onward journeys

Three Hearts

They're clearing the snow from
streets that I walked in another
lifetime I see a shaft of
sun highlight a particular point

where a young tree stands marks
the spot I want to revisit these
streets hand held in shared pockets
away from the histories of home

to travel share in the creation
of the new matched possibilities
a time for combined healing
and re-birth of the ordinary

*It's all about coming to terms
with life and love*

Conker

i.m. David Hurley

They are good for you she
said as dew massed against
the front of shoes

The sunflowers are out at the village Post Office

I gather conker an Autumn
habit for them to gather dust
on window sill

The trees are losing their leaves

That goodness via tablet form
runs through those scarred veins
pumped slow

The tarmac catches the afternoon light

Three movements to fade
a handshake a kiss a wave
fades to white

Catalf

Things will never be the same
again light will angle differently
cold will eat summer

Gone my friend   grief will make her heart burst

Can we go on like this with our hearts tied to the land?

Paths taken guided by Common
Century the alleyways
your territory

Marked indefinitely
the house stands quiet
a mosaic memorial

There is no comfort in this world that's why I love you today

Bedroom chimney shaft
of morning
the mastering of absence

Your shadow will remain
indelible lit from behind
a portal resolution

Must you be on your way?

Poetry and Skin Cream

When the fog lifts and you walk away
I hope that you'll glance over your shoulder
and wave from the built up distance

December foxes and urban fireflies
the cold comfort of a hiding place.

How the season comforts enables
sleep to be disturbed by machines
as frost filters through the night sky

Empty Ring Finger

I notice the earrings first
the heat makes it look like I've a tan

She crosses near the prison
bass drum doubles its beat

city feels like L.A. in August
but this is Liverpool in June

Is love the size of a shoebox?
scratched inside forever etched

birds drift away with the tide
as night drops temperature

remains neon of Hardman Street
advertising refreshment

come on you can dance I'm waiting
with modern modes of communication

Get Well, Mend

raindrops
scroll street lit

white cat
against the wall

startled in headlights

Gus sits stares
at the hedge in blue light

I begin to think about home

gaps between
that gather dust

written to exist
poems need habitat

to be located

I drift to dwell
like roses in the snow

scattered wildly

We Paint While You Sleep

Shortest night these long hours
         a comfort to know while we sleep
the furies gather amongst the dunes

tide and wind sand against
walls of supermarkets

yellow neon bright to sea
patch of non-illumination
a field in North Wales

Dawn rising over rocks off the coast
those rocks belong to all of us

orange sky   cracks appear horizon
drops into day screech of morning birds

all the big trees harbour secrets
and twine is washed up on the shore

In Heels She Feels Closer to God

She stands hand on hip
          surveying
all below angled towards
the northern star

Stellar reaction
amidst the cables
artificiality
leg angled strap slung
top riding high   "California"

pink flowers emit
                the smell of death
like lilies

surrounded by candles

Amongst the detritus
of the Lower East Side

a vigil where green haired girls
compare tattoos
          and share their drugs

until the candles meet their end

Hit so hard
          she sees stars

          and wishes him alive

Into the Blue Again

Stars in amber shapes in violet
summer's final days

the underground gallery
submerged in blue

bag carrying photographing
from parkland

across fields of sculpture
littered with oaks

to shade of deer shelter

be taken and see it's all we
can do

to investigate the bearer
of revelation

the source the light itself

To a Fox

Slumped gutter tied dirt

your signifier hint of white ignored
through jams policed by woods
dotted by bluebells

Scanned noted eyes tired

days start over end prefer
to see movement cross roads
flash like

Sized counted weighed tagged

a unity bond through two colours

dusk with moon shining
lime tree all spriggy
bunched up leaves bats air spiced
with wallflowers pheasant scratching
amongst the daffodils

town jointed union squares

crucifix centre for continental markets
Easter walk of witness

Perhaps there is not one
essence but many perhaps
all you will ever get
is a fleeting impression It's

like trying to catch rain drops
with a fishing net—the mesh
gets wet with the substance of rain
but you can't capture its being
because as soon as the rain stops
falling through the sky it's not raindrops
anymore just polluted water

Back seated car parked

Home for weekend routine changed
weather reigned in footpaths walked

arbour blossom dropping into vanilla
flavoured coffee

at rest

(with thanks to Ursula Hurley)

Knitbone

the process needs assessment
the liquid is dark green
      smells of eucalyptus

a need to be healed

take all the precautions necessary
bathe in lavender foam
reading and trying to unwind

and avoid dreaming of a past
involving ocean views
      at Half Moon Bay
city vistas from the 86th floor
coffee from Peet's
      doughnuts from Krispy Kreme

a time when the future was bright

heat surrounds as pages turn
offering a glimpse into
      the other side of the American Dream

I think about writing
through the difficulty

epically moving this soundtrack

Third Rail

Buttercups spread like fire snakes
         meadows give way to lush green
manicured golf grass

motorway concrete halts spread
disused container   heat contained

enclosures abstract scaffold

in the 1980s on Bidston Moss tip they scavenged
for food

Caution moving trains   production shed
banks of bramble   coolness of tunnel
spotted pink rose   black of bricks

white of platform edge   breeze blocked
paint dripped hushed undergrowth
unused rails   scattered daisies seek the sun

The Bang of the Bee

Tapping at 6.00 a.m. French windows
except I'm not in France

Clouds are low for June yesterday Marta
complained about the weather

The bee tries to gain access flies off in a huff
the tea is slightly milky

The flowers that Antoine bought are
lasting well I think it's the vase

High skirting boards low window frames
a quietness enhanced by foliage

If Rachel was here she'd talk to the bee
and I'd take her for ice cream afterwards

Instead the goldfinch appears bringing
a recognizable song

Framing Poem:
Drinking Champagne from Plastic Glasses

To cap it all the snow came down
what began with gathering material

at the studio ended with deliveries like UPS
and reversing manoeuvres like seasoned cab drivers

in-between Subway coffee and sandwiches
eagle eyes on the ants below
look at those primary colours check that palette

I'm sick of old Liverpool the way it forces elaborative
encoding this retrieval method tires me

If the Liver Birds were to take off the city would crumble

the ring contains the gold from two wedding bands
and an eternity band

Anna's off to Christmassy up the house cuddle the fox
        wrestle the bear
and stomp the fields

Travel through ice-bound Pennines
we skate down the A565

the windows are the oldest part of the building

in parts this place has the feel of America
shoppers fade like frosted neon reflection

By now the paste will have dried John will have locked the
      second floor
the gifts will have been framed and bought

this city around us

the north docks are quite silent three of the four berths
are empty

Carts are Objects
They Are Little Buildings

It is important to heal
       and to hydrate

seek scraps fallen from fruit and veg
seller's barrows

Straight pressed into survival
       doorways home to blankets

Royal Mail Street public land
appears private

Behind the Adelphi Hotel
houses were built on wasteland

repayments are not being met

In Winter take on more hot liquid
wear layers
keep one room warm   stay in it

venture out if only absolutely necessary

soup is a valid form of nutrition

Fog on the West Coast Mainline

Angels fall through the mist
shaped by the sun

she has been here before
like a ghost in me

the oaks of England silhouette

as ice shapes the golden liquid

a beat of heartbreak
is love all that we've got?

sit and ride the down escalator

roll like ink parallel tracks power
north to south to north

distillation of light through
the contained ether

Carfo

Snow light projection
the effect was as if driving
through a blizzard

Regardless of temperature
the stairs were crowded
back streets empty

In Islamabad storms played havoc
with the satellite feeds

Mishal loves the South Asian
summer rain

especially when thinking of January

Amari

How I love the smell of Autumn in the morning.
Wind throws spent leaves in a merry dance,
power cables whistle in time. As the storm
gathers in, a train pulses by on a grey horizon.

A heater clicks in Room 111 of the Days Inn,
Bristol West. Workplace shelf cleared, neutrality
brushed aside. Make a mark! capture the image,
the M5 at its rush-hour best.

Light streaks luminous outside lane. Air-condition
cold swirls through service station view. Nature
and human interaction, hard shoulder borders
ripple with nocturnal creatures.

October mist descends like a shroud, brings evening
on board. Journey through carved country, picturing
the view of cows from bridges, that cross to shelter
and dream of daybreak.

New Cut

A tributary a flow
follow progress line

concrete and boulder
irremovable

trace route map reader
these fields hold stories

refill the glass green and yellow
spring water ice cubes

bridges offer shelter from rain
clamber trackside

store sound
smell tar

Sandy Brook

Scratched buckle tells a tale
despite value loss of sheen
loss of love tin-man heart
needs oil expectation required

Old Canal

Brewery Lane bridge bankside 4.00 a.m.
seven years no memorial no flowers no resting place
as you wish

It doesn't help though

edgelands that change with seasons change with light

not wanting to leave the golden age
walk in feathery rain

Fine Jane's Brook

Booked the plot
the heart is going back

ice-cream vans doves distant traffic
birdsong initial thoughts of Disco Inferno

lost in the mix

it's where I'm from it's where I belong

Leather Barrow's Ditch

Sky like Alice Glass's torn blue tights

From the strawberry picking ground
slow bank pass the Runny's the Swingy
the coal yard

Nice is good except in a poem
Morgan fits so well it's the breathlessness

actually the shade is more like Clementine's
hair at the apartment while drinking Bombay Sapphire

Alley's head cold is raging anybody know an instant cure?

No it's Natasha's leggings at Glastonbury 2009

There is no need for a torch

There is no need for a torch
the whiteness of the fields
allows the eye to settle
spot the amber lights of the horizon
through the swirling snow

Quite what I'm doing here is almost a mystery
walking through the fields to the church
on a Winter's eve

Almost medieval this weather though
the glow of the pub enticing in its simplicity
offers a heightened sense of modernity

Returning past the former houses
of friends long gone
a hint of wood smoke allows
for the collection of memories that evaporate

through the iced tips of hedgerows

Chicken Pig

Location locked firm
        writing machines hedge
view to fields beyond

green and white desk
        chopped firewood an
Autumn testament

first publication tea at five
        comfort of audience
harmony of routine

*

Positioned licensed a new
        order metropolis of
possibility

needled incomprehension
        horizon signifiers
comfort through summer madness

Public art station walks Palanzana
        Unknown Landscape # 3
The Tango Ray and Julie Sea Circle

*

Air-conditioned basement
        monitors surround
postcards shelf stacked

encased metallic blue freed
        hotel furniture resting
place reflections on rye

Greenness of canal bandstand
        rendezvous isolation
jet watching double glazing

                *

Year of death and disease
        cabin walls drip
behind blinds of Winter

Copse lifeless nature redolent
        shut down magnetic voices
recording tape rattled railings

Car park light cast glow
        empty space years end
lock the cabin door

                *

Dreams of Winter Hill
        A Certain Ratio
red letters on the dashboard

flash neon satellite navigation
        time zones a freeway
and city midnight junk

Orange support through fog
       bay lights glimmer
Star Room Dancing a hotel view

Like Geese Calling in the Night

They are out there
       our shining hours await
the softest kisses
       as garden constellations

Yellowing lime tree
       leaves a rooted bond
an apple left on a desk
       rots after six months

Starlit on Exit

the acorns were Catherine's idea

Paper planes white against blue

veins lined like paths
starlit on exit

tide is low
beach huts on concrete

Give Me Blue Paint

The pot is on the waft is irresistible

it feels like summer's return
a car is being valeted under the trees
people are just trying to earn a living

the shrink-to-fits have seen better days
it may be time to get the dye out
extend usage and save on postage or a trip to America

Sometimes I prefer to avoid breakfast it makes the first cup

the third button down is stitched with red thread

It is the finest of details
the kind that emerge after
careful consideration

open the brown paper parcel

follow the arc of the twig
as it heads towards the snow
making an angel of its own

a rocking chair comes to rest
out the window the shimmer of air

as darkness falls defusing light
from across the valley

Dial 9 for an Outside Line

Across rooftops spire cuts
into clear evening sky

common edged technology
amasses through wires

into the chest
            battery powered 6-10 years

shadows fall away
fingerprints are left on desks

ice melts slowly in an engraved glass
flowers sway in the churchyard after dark

basement desk holds mementos
pacemaker amongst the relics

memoirs gather dust

space for unrestricted breath
low light design studio productiveness

dial 9 for an outside line

fading of traffic calm at the junction
new recordings to add to catalogue

roads are flooded passing an impossibility
a smell of autumn eroding at last

the pressure of summer

Common Salt

Share with legends dust cracks
between pavements

Palaces in the sun not just 23rd
street the second time

when optimism burned deep
and transatlantic calls

were for shopping lists

Guiding light persuader you
made me visit the 110th floor

Somebody was watching over us
after shopping tempting as it was

to sit it out and watch shadows
gather and drink coffee

but the memory belongs in this moment
probably forgotten by the lesser ones

Lent

I hear the planet crying   such Teen Angst
withdraw from use

allow for repair a reconstruction of the senses

amidst the sunshine there will be showers

a blue box of magic tricks
modulator synthesis

forty days   forty nights   forty lines

this time of year   available light

precursor to walking city rivers   skimming pebbles

wish for a clearer way
like a leaf circling around the deer shelter

and the poppy towering above the tall grass

9.48 to Euston

Tilt and speed through April green countryside
 here a cocoon of comfort
while the mind is jumble
 think only of today

Frosting Pools
for Eleanor Rees

Homesickness desire for a sense of calm
 quiet reflection and rest
stars reflect in frosting pools
 nesting birds are sleeping sound

19.07 to Lime Street

Such evening light over dark brown fields
 landscape broken with church spires
thoughts turn to her sweet as
 scents from hedgerow blossom

Bara Brith

Ideal for the age of austerity
 soak in tea overnight
fruit speckled bread delicious
 with hot tea and Welsh butter

The Lingering Scent of the North

As old as light from stars
these routes map connections

across hills down urban
corridors until they hit water

like de-freezered ice-cream river
mist rises hiding the source
of a tolling bell a building
shaped like a ship's bow contains

memories of room service and to think
the Liverpool Inner Motorway

would have followed the curvature
past dock walls up north past suburbia

and out back past points of departure
the lights thin the air becomes

cooler and somehow homing pigeons
know to return

M58 poem:
Right Snow Wrong Quantities

There is salt despite being
nowhere near   the sea
it sprays from surface
to screen   we seek the north

and recreation

the hills a white tint legacy
of location   spots of time
the nourishment   of minds

repaired invisibly

such sound landscape matched
sonic cathedrals   made out of ice

Love is undefined   it enters the hall
cloaks itself amongst antiquities
                         amongst the views to the lake
along the stalled grass to the shore

it is looped in piano music in refrains
in dimly lit buildings snow gathered

against dry stone walls   it is here

the air is different
reminiscent of Europe   cloudless
stars   clearer

like gathered polished stones initialled

Snow is in the air
         despite forecast
whispering in naked hedgerows

it arrives   upon departure

The Port

for Chris McCabe and Sarah Crewe

Smoke like thin trees
  some leaves have made it down

I'm not prepared to call this
an Indian summer without
thinking of Beat Happening

Chris is dashing off to Euston
  to catch the train back home

rainy night in the port
  his wife tells him

the beer travels well despite
  the distance

all ports should have a brewery
  for distribution

the lower the light
  the better the glisten

when the chips are hot the gods are mad

outside Euston read the inscription:
E. Paolozzi London 1980
it's written

there

rain drops
  leaves leave imprints

stacked hay sprayed slogans
    red paint

fields rise to brow in readiness
    like flocks gathering material

radio mast horizon
    train tilts away from motorway
follows its route

extended summer late autumn
rain falls but at night

insects are confused

Wear the pen in a pocket
close to the heart

Sodium Darkness

Illuminated like an architect's drawing
technically it's France through the barrier

blue mix within the amber
the black of background

thirteen year stay south of the river
movement to the north

continental escalators slow to stop
somehow it's easier from the north

resurrection on the Euston Road
ghost platforms weed-less secured

somewhere there are footprints
this part of the city is essential

like the lapping tide from the estuary
it rolls and rolls

A Poetry Now

for Tom Raworth

travel through Bostonian dawn
    time shift through messenger hits

UK Duty Paid

Kent was in full autumn foxes
    and pheasants crossing the lanes

trapped in mesh fence
CCTV windows a security hut

Le Monde a US Campus

new classicality a Vegan promoter
    sound-tracking death

Autumn becomes Winter
the first frost

purchasing a Watch Cap
    in anticipation

closed Easter, Thanksgiving Day and Christmas Day

of season accompanied by the swan's call
preparation for the long sleep

Concrete

For Tadao Ando

In cities concrete appears to criticism
Manchester's wall cuts through the gardens

"this is not a pavilion, this is a wall"
"No, it's clearly a pavilion"

"It's not very Manchester" "It is
you know" I think of Joy Division

and men in long overcoats being
photographed on footbridges in snow

inspired formwork poured in place
doesn't look at all   out of place

take shelter trams twist in from suburbs
neon glimmers Pizza Express Anno 2007

across the gardens sparks fly as blue fades
time shimmers across the divide

[acknowledgements to Michael Ashton]

150 W 4ᵗʰ Street

Your menu takes me back
to chilled streets hazed
blue with coffee roasting
landmarks like old friends

we rise from boiling subway
after gridlock forced us
down Bleeker Street into
Macdougall Street and home

where fridge magnets leave
messages

Ice forms in gutters steam
inside windows news stands
exotic titles theatre boards
all viewed through smatterings

of snow turned grey with fumes
and traffic

From the 39th Floor

Streets mapped as if by Haussmann midtown
Polaroid age of colour daily news traffic

increase uptown to extended neon billboards
billowing smoke and steam from the roadway

Almost half a century on the skyline remains
enforced demolition these streets carry histories

There's some nice parts of Manhattan you can
see them from here

Couples in love wandering hand in hand
             flocks of birds in small parks

taking drink in bars grey atmosphere of backrooms
authentic coffee from delis polystyrene cups

Go everywhere by foot exploration a natural way
to Lexington and 52nd Street stand above the subway
             ventilation

Swift Black

to seek a sensual refuge
               in the 20th arrondissement
repair   rebuild   reassess

five star bedding
          somewhere to work
maybe write a letter on headed paper
watch a DVD or read a book

connect to a lifeline
desire elegance and functionality
drink in the bar
lovers of deep melancholic
conversation gather here

candles reveal a desire
a city to be explored
rediscovered to feel loved in

the leaves stick solemnly
to the cobbles by the river
their prints reveal a state of semi-permanence

A Snowy Night in Greenwich Village

The pharmacy neon sign is weakened
I remember leaving Zinc in sub zero temperatures
steam rises from red and white striped funnels
the water towers must be frozen

if only I'd known then what I know now

Amber and Ryan decide to go to Greenwich
Village on a snowy night and emerge from
the subway at 8th and Broadway
the flashlight blurs out the falling flakes

the pea coat I am wearing offers scant protection

Coureur - de - Bois

People get the tree lady coffee
it's the cold

neighbours show
up with hot chocolate
and hot meals

*It's nighttime this is when
the magic starts*

Let's not forget it's an island
you're never far from water

Forget the grid accelerate
concrete to creosote
parcel deliveries
stamped company logo

Bag tied transported
sapped smell of pine

A late night sale in the making?

*No just another group of drunks
out for the night they circled
the giant tree joined their hands
to give it a big hug*

Some things never change

Sudden snowstorms

Celebrity customers

Bizarre requests

It's surreal to see
the city empty just for
an hour or two and then
to be out and see it waking up

They were both nursing cups
of hot water with heavy doses
of Theraflu

We've sort of been in our cave
for about a year
it's time to see the sun

Notes for Tiffany

She has yet to unfold

   like a crisp white bed sheet
her practice is folded at the bottom

   of a drawer

doing absolutely nothing
but keeping the bottom
of the drawer
company

waiting for supplies
canvasses paints books and groceries

she is still without soil and seeds

work from her room
   without concern for whether or not
she has showered or brushed her teeth

roll out of bed start work
   start making
start creating

Give the half of the studio back

wander home

In the jug February's daffodils
open

she has run out of stamps

Manhattan 98

Poster information junction
    a thousand leaves bloom
in a hundred squares

Nothing has changed
    I still love you

Shrinking jeans in a small tub

Are flowers a waning asset?

ask the delivery man

This city of lugging utility rules
    case of vanity mirror intact

make up   made up

Yellow at crossing through mesh
    let's watch the hail

Found negatives
the bridge isn't supported by concrete

there's more than that in this jungle

House red rare time alone
    Nico in Carmine
routes up 23rd

where eight months earlier
    we couldn't afford to sleep

Thrift store blue and green
    you in pink Simpsons sky
allows for breath

like a chopped up piano
    I scatter among low mix
brass instruments

not being magnificent
I'd fallen in the Manhattan
    dawn

Radio

studio apartment pianist
composes notates
  the dinner is delivered

Love is the available transport
courtyard is thoughtful

  loft ballet dancer gives
a low
  warm laugh

the street is fogged in

radio brings silence

Elegiac Stanzas

for Clare Greenhalgh

Embrace this open season
      buds turn skywards
shore sand raked spring an

endless seed of mystery

Decoration comfort zone
      defer descent into dust
deep breathe air a freshness

coppice-like activity of desire

Horizon cleared term-time
      a newness of form
descends blue afternoon

through bold positive thought

Under Sleepers

This city is at its best
　　it is like L.A. but cooler

ship is docked against
altered skyline

gone are the three ugly sisters
those left remain adequately
poised for museums

Albion House
　　　　they called the names
from the second floor balcony

on the tide she leaves
stow the gear

put the kettle on

On Listening to Epic45 Travelling North II

sublime soaked in memory
first hearing its associations
marked shorn fields spires
lazy lanes
trimmed hedges
glockenspiel

My heart forever given over
the bond is blood

she doesn't know it yet
though I see it in her eyes
as if she almost knows

It seems south do you understand
northernness?

like the way this music cuts through

Love flows through a necessity

Light falls through August
at a rapid rate

like the half harvest moon
you will appear to me
across the fields
through the darkness

from the speeding train
through floodlights and municipal work

a value in repeated airings

the grass will be glad of the rain

Swayling

Against the snow the scarf is spectacular it is frozen

Feed the ponies polos an afternoon walk
making own steps heels dance red
bitten fences worn down path

the goat is not in the garden the shed is locked
I'll look for the first sign of flowers
metal has replaced the arching wood

I asked for a replica a photograph will do

Chocolate Soup
for Robert Sheppard

This soup is not for diabetics
this soup is for tea with tea
and sandwich

butternut squash parsnip
and chilli this is both
food and drink wholesome
& nutritious

*You can lose yourself in making soup. The imagination can start
to spiral into uncharted regions, reality can become bearable, even
enjoyable. You can also find yourself in making soup, though what
you find may bore you. It always starts with chopping onions.
Holding back the tears has to be mastered, but once that's done,
onions are the most rewarding vegetable in the world to chop.
Everybody loves the aroma of frying onions. It's what unites all
meals in every kitchen around the world.*

Bill Drummond says

Soup may be the medium
start with onions
a pan large enough
think of Bill Griffiths's vegetable
poems

inspiration comes from
          the most unlikely source

Elly dislikes peas rolling around
          her plate
'though mushy peas would be still'

Peas are good ingredients for soup
they become sweet and offer
texture as the skin sheds and rather

like the broad bean in a Madras curry
they become comforters

of soup and love, the first is the best
Thomas Fuller 1654-1732

Cat Cairn

Dark matches cold
beyond trees light
un-gritted road   tracks spread evenly

sparkle and slide   hit the north pink opaque

The circle pristine foot free
two flasks stand
emptied
tea taken

the sky sits closer

Turrell's signature Michigan State University
for Cristina
alcohol sticks to the glass

here liquid solidifies
trek up takes breath away

she dreams of me and wakes at 4.00 a.m.
some things don't need to be navigated

Acknowledgements

Acknowledgements due to the following publications for previously publishing poems contained in this collection:
Alligator Stew, Fire, The Red Ceilings, Poetry Wales, Thirteen Myna Birds, Unquiet Desperation, Calliope Nerve, Great Works, Neon Highway, Side of Grits, Willows Wept Review, Full of Crow, Gists and Piths, Sunk Island Review, Haiku Scotland, New Aesthetic, Blue and Yellow Dog, The Balloon, The Binturong Review, Psychic Meatloaf, Counter Example Poetics, Leaf Garden, Ditch, Lit Up, Private International Review of Photographs and Texts, Back to the Machine Gun and to BBC Radio Merseyside for broadcasting 'Three Hearts'.

Grateful thanks to the editors and publishers of the following pamphlets where some of the poems were previously published:
'Comfort & Joy' (Ten Pages Press, 2011);
'The Lights will Inspire You' (Full of Crow Press, 2011);
'The Sound of Light Aircraft' (Knives Forks and Spoons Press, 2010);
'The Metaphysics of a Vegetarian Supper' (Differentia Press, 2009);
'Poetry and Skin Cream' (erbacce-Press, 2004 and 2007);
'And the Weary are at Rest' (Sunnyoutside Press, 2008) and
'Carts Are Little Objects They Are Little Buildings' has appeared in *The Robin Hood Book: Verse Versus Austerity* eds. Alan Morrison & Angela Topping Brighton: Caparison, 2012.

Thanks to Robert Sheppard, Scott Thurston, Cliff Yates, Alan Corkish, Tony Frazer, Nichola Marr, Alex Byron, Sarah Crewe, Chris McCabe for the title suggestion, WJ and EM Taylor and Ursula Hurley for keen eyes and helpful suggestions.

Lightning Source UK Ltd.
Milton Keynes UK
UKOW05f1611070813

215008UK00001B/7/P